Artists at Work
Stone

Cheryl Jakab

Smart Apple Media

This edition first published in 2006 in the United States of America by Smart Apple Media.

Smart Apple Media
2140 Howard Drive West
North Mankato
Minnesota 56003

First published in 2006 by
MACMILLAN EDUCATION AUSTRALIA PTY LTD
627 Chapel Street, South Yarra, Australia 3141

Visit our Web site at www.macmillan.com.au

Associated companies and representatives throughout the world.

Copyright © Cheryl Jakab 2006

Library of Congress Cataloging-in-Publication Data

Jakab, Cheryl.
    Stone / by Cheryl Jakab.
    p. cm.—(Artists at work)
    Includes index.
    ISBN-13: 978-1-58340-779-0
    1. Stone carving—Juvenile literature. I. Title.

NB1208.J35 2006
736'.5—dc22   2005057944

Edited by Sam Munday
Text and cover design by Karen Young
Page layout by Karen Young
Photo research by Jes Senbergs
Illustrations by Ann Likhovetsky

Printed in USA

Acknowledgments

The author would like to acknowledge and thank all the working artists and hobbyists who have been quoted, appear, or assisted in creating this book.

The author and the publisher are grateful to the following for permission to reproduce copyright material:

Cover photograph: A Native Eskimo soapstone sculptor carves a soapstone piece, courtesy of Gunter Marx Photography/CORBIS.

Art Archive, p. 17; ArtnetAfrica, p. 24; Coo-ee Picture Library, pp. 4 (bottom right), 10, 13, 22; Corbis, pp. 4 (top), 5, 8, 14, 15, 16 (left), 19, 20, 21, 25; Henry Moore Foundation, p. 11; Image Library, p. 4 (bottom left); Lochman Transparencies, p, 9; Lonely Planet Images, p. 23; Photos.com pp. 16 (right), 18; Quest Gallery, pp. 26, 27; Sarah Saunders, p. 6.

While every care has been taken to trace and acknowledge copyright, the publisher tenders their apologies for any accidental infringement where copyright has proved untraceable. Where the attempt has been unsuccessful, the publisher welcomes information that would redress the situation.

Please note

At the time of printing, the Internet addresses appearing in this book were correct. Owing to the dynamic nature of the Internet, however, we cannot guarantee that all these addresses will remain correct.

Contents

Stone artists   4

What is stone?   6

Stone work   8

Focus on technique Cutting and polishing   12

Stone history   14

Stone treasures   16

Case study Taj Mahal   18

Where stone artists work   20

Case study Constantin Brancusi   21

Showing stone artworks   22

Stone artists' groups   24

Case study Inuit stone carving   26

Project Make an Inuit-style carving   28

Stone timeline   30

Glossary   31

Index   32

Glossary words

When a word is printed in **bold**, you can look up its meaning in the Glossary on page 31.

Stone artists

Marble is a smooth kind of stone often used to make statues.

Look at these different artworks made by stone artists. Stone artists are people who design and make artworks with **minerals** from the earth. Stone artists include people who work as stonemasons, architects, sculptors, jewelers, and **lapidaries**. Stone artists work stone that may be hard or soft, large or small, colorful, shiny, or dull into a wide variety of forms including:

- huge sandstone buildings
- sculpted marble figures
- colorful **gemstone** jewelry
- perfectly cut and polished diamonds
- polished decorative stone ornaments
- carved **cameo** and **intaglio** brooches and rings

Stone is used to make buildings because it is a long-lasting material.

Carvings made from stone can be any size.

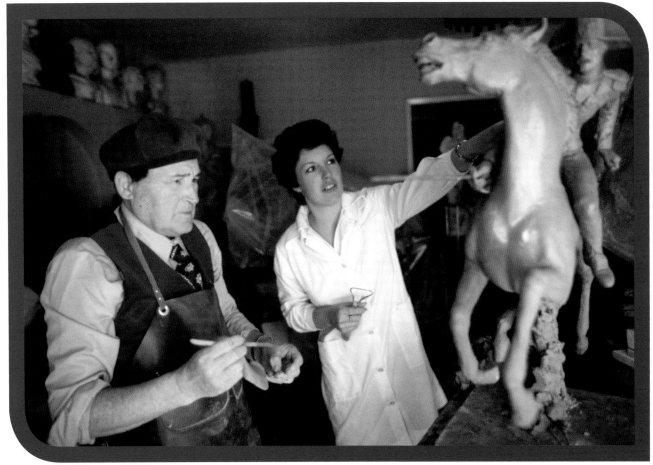

Using Stone

No matter what they make, stone artists need to be skilled at creating, choosing, and shaping stone. In this book, you will find the answers to these questions and more:

- ▶ What do artists need to know about stone to use it creatively?
- ▶ How do the chosen stones help the artist express their ideas?
- ▶ What is it that artists like about stone as a **medium** for art?
- ▶ How and where do stone artists work?

▲ Applying the finishing touches to a sculpture.

"The marble not yet carved can hold the form of every thought the greatest artist has."
Michelangelo, Italian artist

What is stone?

The term "stone" describes any rock or large lump of mineral. Most stone consists of **sediments** that have been mixed together and changed with time. Many different minerals may be pressed tightly together in stones, although some stone can contain only one mineral.

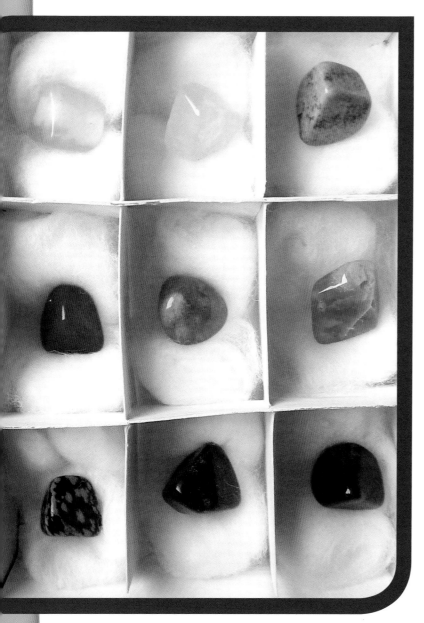

Classifying stone

Stone or rock is classified according to how it forms. Stone or rock is constantly being formed, exposed, and eroded. The three main types of stone are:

1. **igneous** rocks that form from magma and larva
2. **sedimentary** rocks that form from sediments
3. **metamorphic** rocks that are rocks changed by heat and pressure

Crystals

The minerals that make up stone are in one of seven crystal shapes. Each type of mineral takes one of these shapes. Ornamental stones are usually minerals that form into large crystals. They are described as **precious** stones (such as diamond or ruby) and gemstones (including lapis, onyx, and opal).

Types of Stone

Stone	Type	Formation	Characteristics	Uses
granite	igneous stone	formed within the earth from magma	• mixture of colors • coarse-grained rock	• building material
basalt	igneous stone	formed when lava is cooled and becomes solid	• heavy rock • fine-grained	• building material
obsidian	igneous stone	natural glass formed by rapidly cooled magma	• shiny glass • sharp-edged	• early tools
sandstone and claystone	sedimentary stone	formed by layers of sediments being pressed tightly together	• color depends on grains in sediments	• building material
limestone	sedimentary stone	formed by water seeping through rocks and dissolving chemicals which then build up to form the stone	• soft rock • often contains layers	• building material
quartzite	metamorphic stone	the **pure** form of the mineral quartz, the major mineral in granite	• can be white or colored • hard crystal	• jewelry (gold is found in **seams** of quartz)
marble	metamorphic stone	changed limestone formed by the mineral calcite	• can be a range of colors • hard rock • polishes to a smooth surface	• building material and decoration
flint	metamorphic stone	lumps found in chalk or limestone soils	• hard rock • breaks to a sharp edge	• used for axes, knives, and other tools

Stone work

▼ Traditional stone carving methods are still used today.

Stone can be formed from different minerals and in different ways. Stone artists use these differences to choose and shape stone for particular uses. Many traditional techniques and styles have been developed since prehistoric people first started to use stone as simple tools. Modern artists continue to explore and find new ways to work stone.

Creating with Stone

When creating with stone, the artist must choose from the large number of stone types, working methods, and tools available. Sometimes new techniques and choices in stone become popular and are copied to become new trends.

Advantages of working with stone

Artists enjoy working with stone for many reasons:

- ▶ **permanence** — stone lasts for a very long time unchanged
- ▶ **holds shape** — stone is very strong
- ▶ **color** — large range of colors to choose from
- ▶ **texture** — stones formed from different minerals have different textures, from soft as soapstone to hard as diamond
- ▶ **pattern** — patterns in stone vary depending on the minerals within them
- ▶ **luster** — stone can give a natural shine to surfaces which can be brought out by polishing

🔺 Stones can be made up of different textures and colors.

"Well worked stone invites you to touch and stroke. It is cool and soft and lustrous."
Henry Moore,
English sculptor

Stone artists today

Today, many stone artists are reviving traditional techniques from the past as well as developing new ways of working stone. The variety of colors and textures of building stones and precious stones are used by architects and designers to great effect.

Precious stones

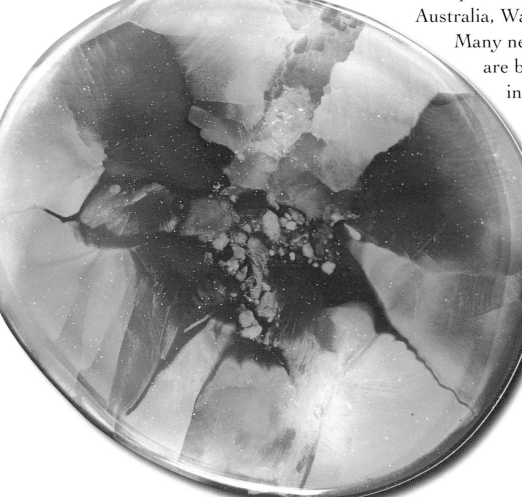

Opals can have a colorful natural appearance.

In recent years, there have been changes in the use and value of precious stones. Opal was used as a gemstone for many centuries but was not considered to be very precious. Today, more types of opal are being used in jewelry. The finest opals are found chiefly in Australia, Wales, and Mexico. Many new opal designs are being developed in these countries. Black opal, found only at Lightning Ridge, Australia, is considered more precious than diamond.

Traditional stone, new techniques

Every type of stone that has been used throughout history is still in use today. The new tools available for working stone mean that artists have been able to develop new techniques.

Power tools can easily cut and shape even the hardest stone. Tools such as power saws and drills make new techniques possible.

In Ancient Rome, marble was used in large sculptures and as a common building stone. It is now very expensive and generally only used for smaller items or special buildings. Huge pieces of travertine and harder stones can now be sculpted into smooth flowing shapes using modern power tools.

"When you carve (stone) you are dealing with the absolute final piece. The practical problems are greater than those you would have with casting in metal."
Henry Moore, English sculptor

🔺 This sculpure, by Henry Moore, was made in travertine because the light color makes it stand out in front of this building.

Cutting and polishing

Experts in cutting and polishing precious stones are called lapidaries. Stones that have been found or mined need to be cut into fragments and polished to expose fine jewels. When taken from the ground, most gemstones look dull. Splitting the stone reveals the color and luster inside. Skilled cutting and polishing is needed to make best use of each stone. The oldest method of shaping and polishing stone is to rub two stones together. Modern lapidaries have a wide range of modern tools but can also use old techniques.

Popular cuts

The earliest gemstones were cut into simple shapes but later lapidaries experimented with more complex cutting. Expert gem workers explore precious stones such as diamond to find any faults and work them into the shape to bring out the best from each individual stone.

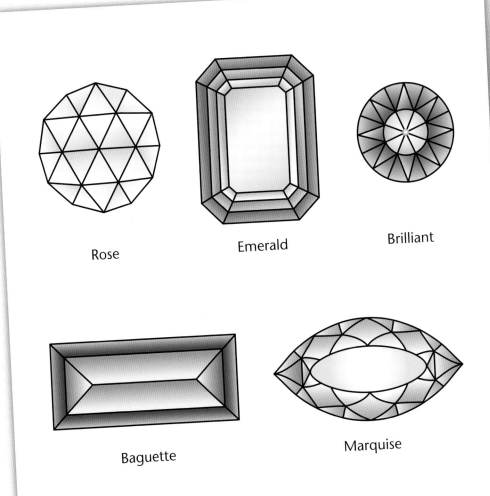

Rose

Emerald

Brilliant

Baguette

Marquise

12

⬤ This shows amethyst in its cut, polished, and uncut form.

Tumbling Stone

Tumbling is a process in which small pieces of stone can be polished by machine. Mineral fragments are tumbled in a drum with finer and finer grades of grit. This smooths and polishes the surface of the stone. Various types of stone are suitable for tumbling. Some of the most commonly used include amethyst, agate, quartz, tiger eye, blue aventurine, and amazonite.

The Artist Speaks

"The violet color in the type of quartz called amethyst occurs unevenly making each stone different."
**Jenine Thelfel,
Teacher/Gemstone collector and worker**

Stone history

People have worked stone since prehistoric times. In fact, the earliest period of human culture is known as the "Stone Age." In the Stone Age, tools were made of stone, bone, antler, or wood. The term Stone Age refers to the time before metals were made into tools. Some very impressive stone artworks were made by Stone Age peoples including standing stones in Europe.

⏷ This hammer head was found in Italy and dates from the Stone Age.

Carving stone

The process of carving stone began when people first made tools. Carving stone is a slow process where the artist cuts away pieces of the stone until they are happy with the result. Spectacular stone carvings were made by ancient cultures, including the famous Easter Island standing figures.

Iron tools for stonework

Once iron tools became available during the Iron Age, stonework became slightly easier but was still a slow process. Today, modern tools such as the **pneumatic** hammer have replaced the stoneworker's traditional wooden mallet and iron hammer.

Great Stone traditions

There are many similarities in ancient stonework traditions across the world. There are also differences due to the use of local ideas, techniques, and the stone types that were available. For example:

- ▶ where flint was readily available, small but strong cutting tools could be made

- ▶ different ancient groups developed techniques for **quarrying**, working, and moving massive stones

- ▶ marble from different areas contains different minerals, giving a range of colors, patterns, and uses

- ▶ some locations contain a natural glass called obsidian which makes fine objects and cutting tools

- ▶ jade was available in the east and became a valued gemstone

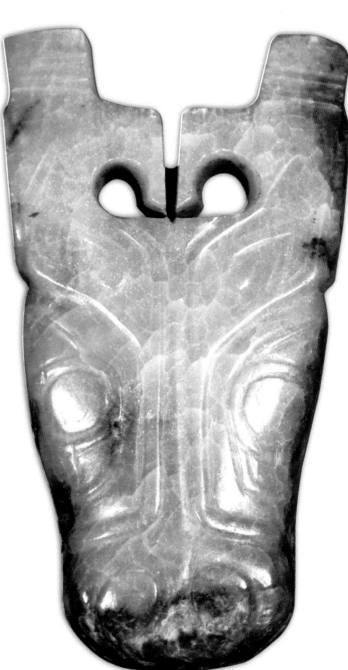

▶ This jade sculpture of a horse's head dates from around 1045–771 B.C.

Stone treasures

Over the years, stone artists have created many different pieces. Some are considered valuable treasures.

Skara Brae is situated on an island off the coast of Scotland. It was discovered in 1850 and is the best-preserved Stone Age village in northern Europe. All the houses, beds, and furniture are made of stone. The site was continuously occupied for approximately 600 years (around 3100 B.C.–2500 B.C.).

Between 200 and 1000 A.D., the people who lived on Easter Island made around 1,000 standing figures. They are called *"ahu moai"* by Polynesians and were carved using adzes, axe-like tools made of igneous rock. About 100 statues still stand on the island.

🔺 The entire village of Skara Brae is a valuable stone artwork.

◀ These giant stone statues were built on Easter Island. Nobody knows the reason why.

The Elgin Marbles

The Elgin Marbles is a collection of ancient Greek marble sculptures made by the Greek master Phidias in around 500 B.C. They were cut from the Parthenon in Athens and taken to London in 1806 by Thomas Bruce, seventh Earl of Elgin. They are now held in the British Museum. The marbles were the first examples of classical Greek sculpture to be seen in England. Elgin purchased the sculptures to prevent them being broken up to make building materials. The British government has been criticized for taking these national treasures away from Greece. They have been asked by the Greek government to return them.

⬤ The Elgin Marbles are extremely detailed stone carvings.

CASE STUDY
Taj Mahal

One of the most famous stone treasures is the Taj Mahal in India. The Taj Mahal is a prime example of Indian-Islamic or Mogul art.

The Taj Mahal is a mausoleum (a stately tomb) made of assorted kinds of marble that took 20,000 workers 20 years to build. It is constructed mainly of white marble decorated with gems. The tomb, which is over 240 feet (73 m) high, is decorated with inscriptions and carved images. It is raised on a square podium with a tower at each corner.

The architect of the Taj Mahal is unknown, but experts suggest that they may have been Persian or Turkish.

▶ The detailed stone artwork of the Taj Mahal makes it a popular tourist attraction.

Shah Jahan ordered the Taj Mahal to be built for his wife, known as Mumtaz Mahal, who died in 1631.

Where stone artists work

Stone artists work in a workshop. The workshop a stone artist needs depends on the type and size of stone being worked. Different stone artists work different types of stone ranging from small gems through to giant blocks.

Gemstone studio

Gem and precious stone artists often have small studios with good lighting, magnifiers to help with the detailed work, and tools such as gem saws, drills, and tumblers.

Large stone studio

The space needed for artists to work large pieces of stone must be large, light, and preferably airy. Giant blocks can be delivered on trucks, moved using cranes, and worked using power tools. Some stone artists still keep old chisels and wooden mallets ready for use, though power tools are a great help when carving out large pieces of stone.

◀ The tools a stone artist uses must be heavy and strong in order to carve out stone.

CASE STUDY
Constantin Brancusi

Constantin Brancusi is considered one of the greatest sculptors of the 1900s. Brancusi's simple stone forms were based on African and prehistoric sculpture. He polished his sculpted shapes over a number of years to develop a deep lustrous finish. To Brancusi, his studio was his home. Towards the end of his life, he chose to stay and die in his studio.

Artist profile

Constantin Brancusi (1876–1957) was born in Romania but moved to Paris in 1904. It was there that he met and worked with other famous modern artists including Auguste Rodin. Brancusi worked with metal and wood as well as stone. His work has influenced modern ideas in sculpture, painting, and industrial design.

The Artist Speaks

"It is not the doing of things that is difficult. What is difficult is getting into the right mood to do them."
Constantin Brancusi, artist

Showing Stone artworks

Stone art needs to be shown to allow the public to admire the artist's skills in choice of stone and technique. Artists' festivals and shows are a popular way of exhibiting works.

Stone festivals

Places where special types of stone are found, mined, and quarried often display finished works in the local stone. Yowah in Queensland, Australia is known for its beautiful and unique opals. "Yowah nuts" are pieces of ironstone with opal deposits in their centers. Like all opals, no two pieces are identical. The Yowah Opal Festival Designer Jewelry Competition commenced in 1997 to promote Australia's national gemstone. World class museum specimens of nut opal, opalized wood, and boulder opal are also on display in Yowah. Visitors come to search for opals, take part in community activities, and purchase opal jewelry during the festival.

Making a living as an artist

Some stone artists, including stonemasons and gem workers, make a living by carving and cutting stone. Many use modern tools to help them work efficiently, but the results they achieve are, in many ways, very traditional. Stone artists can earn a living by cutting stone for jewelry, making marble tabletops, and carving headstones.

Production items and artworks

David McDonald works as an expert stonemason but also creates production items. These are stone items that are relatively cheap for the public to buy. By selling them, he can afford to work on his expensive artworks that take more time to design and make. He also teaches his craft at the local high school to add to his income.

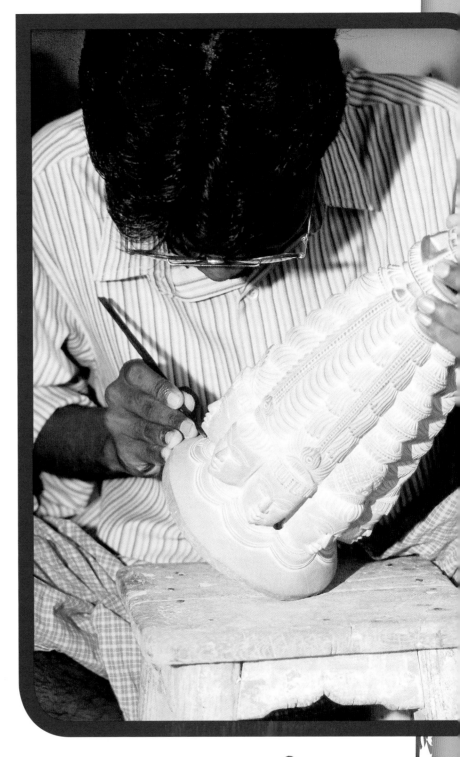

Some stone artworks can take a long time to make.

The Artist Speaks

"I like to teach, to share my skills, but I prefer doing my own art when I can."
David McDonald, stonemason and sculptor

Stone artists' groups

There are many groups that stone artists can join to share ideas with other artists, hobbyists, and interested people.

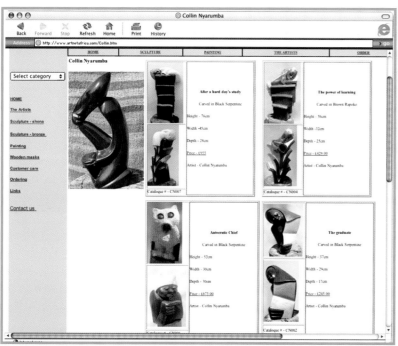

Online groups

Many groups communicate and sell their artworks online. Internet access allows people everywhere to learn about and buy their art.

"Shona" is a style of stone art from Zimbabwe, Africa. The Zimbabwe sculptors work with their local stone, such as springstone. The artwork they produce is displayed on their Web site where it can be seen and bought by anyone in the world.

"The rocks themselves emerge from the quarry like sculptures formed by nature over millions of years and are often a source of inspiration to the artist."
Nicolas Mukomberanwa, artist

◀ The Artnet Africa Web site has many examples of Shona stone artworks.

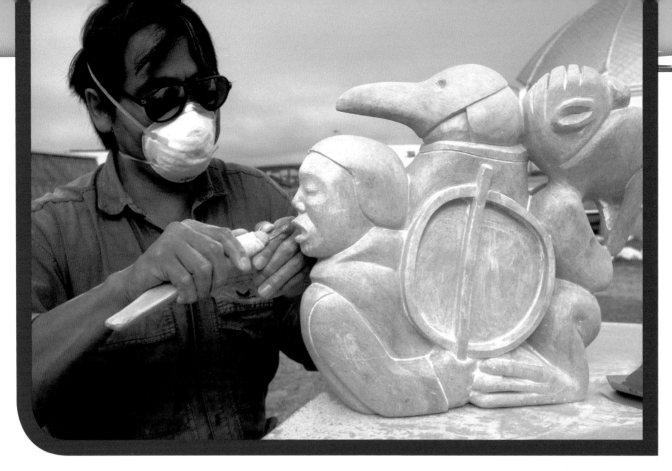

Issues for Stonework artists

Sharing ideas includes learning about health, safety, and the environmental and cultural impacts of working with stone.

Health and Safety

Stoneworkers must protect themselves against inhaling dust and must learn about other hazards involved with their work. They must also wear appropriate clothing and safety equipment such as masks and goggles.

Environmental and cultural impacts

Stoneworkers need to be aware that collecting and quarrying stone can have damaging environmental and cultural impacts. Many stones, including diamonds, are mined by poorly-paid or slave workers.

Some of Australia's most important fossils are made of solid opal. They are often cut up for jewelry or illegally sold overseas. **Paleontologists** often attend opal festivals in order to find such fossils unearthed by opal hunters.

🔺 If you work with stone, you need to protect your eyes and your lungs.

"Opalized fossils are nature's own works of art."
Joe Vida, opal collector

CASE STUDY
Inuit stone carving

The indigenous people of the Arctic, or Inuits, make stone carvings mostly of animals that live in the Arctic. The small sculptures are known for their beauty and strong images. The poses and the small sizes are the two main features of Inuit carving. Though the shapes are simple, the carving is very carefully done. This is to bring out the colors and shapes of the original stone.

Traditionally, these carvings were made in ivory but today they are made in soapstone. Soapstone is the common name for the mineral steatite. It is a very soft stone which is a grey-green or brown color and is the most common form of **talc**.

🔻 This sculpture, by Jonas Faber, is called *Blanket Toss*.

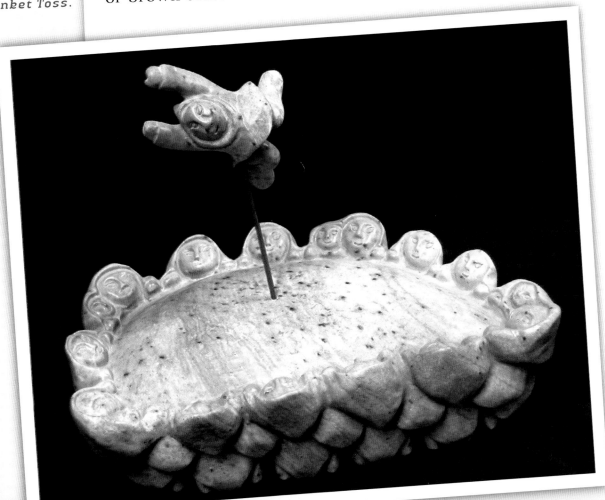

Inuit carving history

The Inuit are the native people of the Canadian Arctic from places such as Cape Dorset, Greenland, and Baker Lake. They live a unique way of life, surviving in the harsh frozen north. Inuit tools have been well-made and decorated by carving since prehistoric times. Traditionally, ivory from walruses and whales was the material used for carving. It was fashioned into figurines representing animals and people as well as being used to make tools.

Around 1950, the Canadian government encouraged the carving and sale of sculptures made in soapstone. Sale of these sculptures creates money for both the artist and the Inuit community.

⬢ Many Inuit sculptures are of animals, such as this one called *Musk Ox*.

PROJECT
Make an Inuit-style carving

Inuit soapstone carvings are smooth, simple shapes. Carving a block to create a sculpture is a "subtractive" method of working. This means that material is removed to create the sculpture. A block of clay can be used for this but should only be worked by pulling and cutting pieces away. Never add pieces back to the block or push the material into shape.

What you need:

- a block of soft stone (such as soapstone, plaster, or clay) about 5 inches by 6 inches by 4 inches (12 cm by 15 cm by 10 cm)

- a butter knife

- water

- a sharp pencil or stick

What to do:

1. Create drawings from every angle on the clay or soapstone with the pencil. (You could draw an Arctic animal such as a seal, dolphin, polar bear, or walrus.)

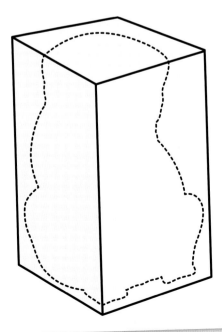

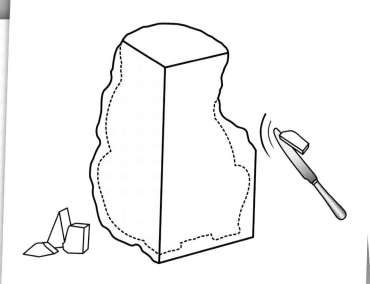

2. Pull or cut stone away from the block with the butter knife. Remember to never add pieces to the block.

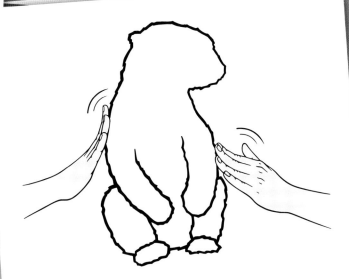

3. When you have cut away as much stone as you can, shape and smooth it by hand until your animal appears.

4. Smooth the piece with water.

5. Add small details with a sharpened stick or pencil point. Use basic lines for details such as eyes and claws.

Stone timeline

B.C.

2 500 000 Early Paleolithic era—creation of earliest stone tools, which have been found in sites in Ethiopia

350 000 Stone axes shaped

180 000 Middle stone age era starts

45 000 Small stone spearheads made

40 000 Middle stone age era ends

30 000 Paintings made on rock surfaces, such as cave walls

20 000+ Late Paleolithic era—carved stone statuettes created in Europe

17 000 Carved and polished sandstone lamps created

8500 Palaeolithic period ends

8000+ Neolithic carvings in stone made in Africa, Asia, and Australia

4500 Large stone monuments created

4000 Jade carving in China

3100 Egyptian Old Kingdom create pyramids

700 Greek sculpture and building begins

447 Work commenced on the classic Greek building, the Parthenon

221 Great Wall of China begun by Qin Shi Huang, the first Emperor of the Qin Dynasty

A.D.

0 Diamond used as a tool by the Chinese for engraving and cutting jade

70 Colosseum built in ancient Rome

120 Pantheon built in ancient Rome

200 Easter Island inhabited and statues built

1631 Taj Mahal built

1806 Elgin Marbles sculptures taken from Athens to London

1861 Pneumatic drill developed for cutting into stone

1866 First diamonds discovered in southern Africa

1905 Brancusi moves to Paris to begin modern sculpture works

1950s Inuit artists begin to use soapstone

1960s Zimbabwe stone sculpture first gained fame

Glossary

cameo a small piece of carving in stone with colored layers

gemstone mineral that is considered beautiful, may be colorful

igneous formed from molten material

intaglio stone with design cut on its surface

lapidaries experts in cutting and polishing precious stones

lustrous shines by reflecting light

medium material used

metamorphic changed by heat or pressure

minerals natural non-living material, obtained from the ground

paleontologists scientists who work on extinct and fossilized animals and plants

pneumatic operated by wind or compressed air

precious highly valued

pure made of one substance, not mixed

quarrying mining stone from the earth

seams joins

sediments layers formed by small particles

talc the softest kind of stone

Index

A

ancient Greek stonework 17

B

basalt 7
black opal 10
Brancusi, Constantin 21
building stones 4, 7, 10, 11

C

claystone 7
crystal 6, 7
cutting stone 12–13, 15, 23

D

decorative stone 4, 7
diamonds 4, 6, 9, 10, 25

E

Easter Island 14, 16, 30
Elgin Marbles 17
environment 25

F

flint, 7, 15
fossils, opalized 25

G

gemstones 4, 6, 10, 12–13, 15, 18, 20, 22
granite 7

I

igneous rocks 6, 7, 16
Inuit carving 26–27, 28–29

J

jade 15
jewelry 4, 7, 10, 22, 23, 25

L

lapidaries 4, 12
limestone 7

M

marble 4, 5, 7, 11, 15, 17, 18, 23
metamorphic rock 6, 7
Moore, Henry 9, 11

O

obsidian 7, 15
opal 6, 10, 22, 25

P

Parthenon 17
polishing stone 9, 12–13
precious stones 6, 10, 20

Q

quarrying 15, 25
quartzite 7

R

Rodin, Auguste 21

S

safety 25
sandstone 4, 7
sedimentary rocks 6, 7
Shona sculpture 24
soapstone 9, 26, 27, 28
standing stones 14, 16
Stone Age 14

T

Taj Mahal 18–19
texture of stone 9, 10
tools 7, 8, 11, 14, 15, 16, 20, 23, 27
travertine sculpture 11

Z

Zimbabwe sculpture 24